Family Frugal Living

Financial Stability for the Present and the Future

By: Katherine Owens

9781635011531

PUBLISHERS NOTES

Disclaimer – Speedy Publishing LLC

This book was originally printed before 2014. This is an adapted reprint by Speedy Publishing LLC with newly updated content designed to help readers with much more accurate and timely information and data.

Speedy Publishing LLC

40 E Main Street, Newark, Delaware, 19711

Contact Us: 1-888-248-4521

Website: http://www.speedypublishing.co

REPRINTED Paperback Edition: ISBN: 9781635011531

Manufactured in the United States of America

DEDICATION

This book is dedicated to my family, to Alfred and Sophia. You always inspire to do more and be at my best.

TABLE OF CONTENTS

CHAPTER 1- HOW TO DEAL WITH FAMILY'S EXPENSES

Family budgeting is very different from the budget requirements of a couple. The needs of a family unit differ greatly from that of a couple without the commitments of having children. Get all the info you need here.

A good and fully comprehensive family finance planning exercise should ideally include items such as dreams, goals, resources and responsibilities of the entire family unit.

This is to ensure all possible bases are cover for the long term planning, thus creating a better overview of the future direction the family should take.

This is also a good way to design the path and work toward the goals set as a family unit. The positive element often enjoyed by this form of planning would include all parties working together and gaining good and practical experiences along the way.

Family Frugal Living

In a lot of cases, the planning of the family budget both in long term and short term formats help to bring the family closer and more capable of handling hiccups along the way.

Family finance planning basics should also ideally take on the element of creating a comfortable leeway for unwanted surprises that are almost certain to happen along the way as the family grows and evolves.

Learning how inspire the family to go along with the expenses prepared is also another important element that can be experienced with the planning exercise.

The entire family will learn to adapt the respective needs and indulgences according to the financial plan drawn. Having discussions and being clear on the financial situation of the family will help instill a sense of responsibility with each family member thus ensuring all work as one unit to make the financial commitment of the family manageable.

The other benefit of family financial planning is also to get the children involved at a very early age, in the various components, commitments and sacrifices the parents would be making on their behalf so that they are able to enjoy a better quality of life.

Always Set a Goal

Getting the family involved at some level of the family financial planning and goal settings will be beneficial to all parties, especially the kids, as they will be able to see firsthand just what it entails to run a family successfully and comfortably.

The perseverance and commitment needed to create a suitable and workable family financial plan will also create a new appreciation by the children for the parents for their willingness to share the fruits of their labor with their children.

Ideally this should be achieved through the arranging of a family meeting to work out the details of the financial goals for the family unit. The following should be some of the elements included in the process of the family meeting for finance planning:

A meeting should be called to discuss the aspirations and goals the family should be working towards as a unit. There should be some level of encouragement for all participating members of the family to be able to express their own individual opinions without reservations.

The key to raising children who are conscious and careful about spending habit is to inculcate very early on in life the merits of budgeting and sticking to the budget designed.

Items such as college funds, car upgrades, large house expenses, retirement funds should all be discussed and clearly outlined for all the members to be encouraged to understand the general commitments of the family income.

Getting the entire relevant document such as financial records and then taking the time to evaluate the financial situation honestly will help greatly in the eventual financial planning stage.

Getting all the family members to be willing to eliminate any unnecessary expenses and frivolous spending is also another positive attitude to encourage through the family meeting.

Do a Self-Check Balance

It would be a good idea to practice periodic financial evaluation for the better understanding of the family's financial standing. This is also important; as it will help the family makes the necessary adjustments should there be a need for such changes.

The net worth of a family is always changing and this is mostly due to outside factors that are beyond the control of the family unit.

Therefore periodic evaluation exercises will help the parents better adjust to these changes and make informed decisions of the future of the family's financial standing.

Sometimes this may include the need to make some cut backs on spending or it may also present some positive saving of which the family may decide to enjoy immediately, or even the prospect of reinvesting any access finances for further gain.

All these decisions can only be done when the whole family is committed to positively contributing to the general finances of the family.

When the help of the whole family is enlisted, any small progress or saving can have quite a liberating effect on the family unit as a whole, as it will help to show the positive results of a family working together for the better good of all.

The motivation that can be gotten out of the family unit being able to manage their finances will is also another positive outcome from this type of family cooperation.

Through the evaluation process of the current financial standing of the individual and the family unit as a whole, other decisions on investment can be made.

If the financial situation allows for a bigger investment portfolio without adversely affecting the current spending power of the family, then such opportunities should be capitalized upon.

However as in all commitments, some caution should be exercised, so as not to over extend one's self.

Chapter 2- Put your Minds Together When Doing Family Budgeting

Sometimes after and evaluation has been done on the family's financial situation, it is found that some changes needs to be made in order for the family to function comfortable without getting into debts. This would require an in depth study of the current spending habits of the family and also reviewing where changes can be made.

The following are some suggestions on how to go about successfully eliminating extra spending without causing undue inconvenience and stress:

Perhaps the first step to initiate would be to compile a list on exactly how the income is being spent.

By determining where the money is being spent, the individual or the family unit will be able to work as a team to identify areas where cut backs are possible and workable.

Once these areas have been identified, the next step would be to actually start making the changes as soon as possible so that immediate overall financial commitments can be decreased.

This would include unnecessary purchases and indulgences that are no longer totally necessary and considered frivolous. The most effective and quick way to being spending under control would be to go shopping with a list compiled of needs rather than wants, and to diligently stick to the list no matter what bargains are available for items not on the list.

Cutting down on entertainment, especially when it is done in an expensive manner is another way to eliminate extra spending. Instead of going out on the town, arrange to have home parties where everyone chips in for food and drinks.

This will not only be an adventurous way of entertaining but would probably be better than some noisy nightclub or expensive restaurant where the bill does not really justify the food ordered.

Having Fun for Less

Although some people may scoff at the idea of "cheap fun", this is often the most enjoyable time people will attest to experiencing. The idea is to be able to have fun without the whole episode costly such a huge amount of money that the possibility of chalking up debts is very real indeed.

The following are some great ways to have fun without breaking the bank:

It is not always necessary to stay home to have cheap fun. There are places the family unit can go together without actually having to incur a lot of costs.

Family Frugal Living

One of the most popular ways would be to go on a picnic. Packing food from home would be the first step in saving cost and licking a location that is both safe and conducive yet near enough not to incur transportation costs would be another plus.

Going on a nature hike is also another cheap way to have fun. Here the family unit will be able to enjoy the exercise together and at the same time learn to appreciate the outdoors and all its many fascinating elements it has to offer for free.

If the family unit is very fond of reading, a trip to the library where hours of reading fun can be experienced for free is another option to enjoy.

This would be cost effective as purchasing material to read can be rather expensive and not really worth the cost it can chalk up in the long run. For those who are culturally inclined, going to the museum and various cultural exhibits would also be comparatively cost effective.

Other activities such as kite flying, going to the beach, walking in the park, playing outdoor games can all be good and cheap, yet great family building activities to indulge in.

Work as a Team

Being able to achieve some level of being financially in sync as a couple is very beneficial to any relationship. Couples already have to face a lot of challenges without having the extra burden of having to contend with family finances.

The following are some suggestions on how to go about finding some common ground for the purpose of ensuring financial possibilities of getting everything in sync:

Perhaps the first step or exercise to attempt would be to disclose any and all financial records. This is the best way to start as both parties will be able to work out honestly where and how the money is coming in and going out.

Understanding this process will also allow the couple to make all the necessary adjustment to ensure there are no future financial disputes within the relationship.

It is very important to be forth coming and very honest at this stage about each other financial credentials.

Once this is clearly mapped out, the next step of discussion and initiating financial goals can be tackled. Discussing future financial goals will also create a stronger bond of cooperation if both parties are agreeable to the goals set.

Working towards these goals can be a very pleasant experience especially if both parties are equally committed.

Once the goals are set, the couple can then move on to making their own financial budgeting agenda.

Here too the couple would need to work together to help each other have a better hold on their commitments and spending power. It is usually easier to budget when there is a check and balance format in place to guide the individual along.

Respecting each other's needs for certain indulgences is also another important element to be conscious off when trying to stay in sync with each other financially. Therefore it would be a good idea not to be to controlling in this area.

The most obvious result of not being financially savvy would be the chances on incurring huge debts would be very high indeed. However it should be noted that with a little thought and help, it is possible to keep one's finances in order, so as not to be burdened in the future with mounting problems.

There are a lot of dangers that the individual or family unit will encounter along the way if there is no control or format laid out for financial order.

One of the dangers would be to fall so far into debt, that it would be very difficult and sometimes impossible to get out from under these acuminated debts.

In some cases there is simply no recourse that can be taken other then resorting to declaring one's self a bankrupt. This is the worst possible scenario to be in, therefore before matters reach anywhere near this level, step should be taken to minimize spending.

When finances are not in order, is would be impossible to spend wisely as there would not really be any clear list on what and where the priority for spending should be.

The danger would be to simply and blindly spend on everything and anything without keeping proper records or tracking the spending habits, thus causing a lot of damage to the financial credibility of the individual. This of course will eventually affect the family and their needs too.

When finances are not in order, there is also the possibility of losing the current lifestyle enjoyed, simply because those responsible for payments can no longer make them. This pressure will not only cause the individual to be frustrated but will also contribute to severely damaging any relationships and family units.

CHAPTER 3- FULL GRASP OF FAMILY BUDGETING

Let's face it the high cost of living in today's society, wherever you may be, has made budgeting a priority among many families.

In today's inflationary world, nothing is more important than knowing how to wisely spend the somewhat meager income that you bring home.

Did you know that.......financial problems usually arise due to lack of proper budgeting skills, or failure to stick to the budget you create? No matter how much income you may have, it is still important to keep track of your assets, liabilities, earnings and expenses.

It is ironic but a person who earns thousands will have the same problems with the person who earns by the hundreds. Most often, different kinds of people, with diverse income levels, have budgeting problems. Others, who may have been successful in creating a budget, usually fail to stick to the budget that they have worked so hard to put in place.

What exactly is a budget?

A budget simply refers to a financial plan that takes the incoming and outgoing monetary resources into consideration. A good budget should not only mean a balance or equity between income and expenditures. It also means lesser expenses, and making an allowance for savings.

Let's say you earn a thousand dollars per month to begin planning your budget you should map out all the necessary expenses you will have during a month such as your house payment, food and transportation. What remains after you deduct your total expenses from your income is your savings.

Sounds simple enough right?

What you do with your savings will make a difference later on, when the need arises. You can choose to keep your savings in a piggy bank or place it in a bank where there is minimum interest rate but at least your money is safe from you and from intruders. Once your savings grows you can enlist the services of a financial adviser who can give you higher-yielding investment options.

Now let's go over a feud tips to make sure that you keep within the family budget that you set:

1. Maintain a logbook where you can list your income and expense account on a weekly or monthly schedule.

2. Buy your groceries at one time. To do this, make a list of all the things that you would need for your target period and purchase

them at one time. Sometimes, there are discounts if you buy by the dozen so take advantage of this.

3. Avoid going to the supermarket and shops if you do not need to buy necessary items. This will keep you from making unnecessary purchases and keep you from straying away from your budget.

Don't Go Overboard

Budget is basically a money plan, outlining your financial goals. By having a budget, you will be able to establish and regulate your funds, set and achieve your financial objectives, plus make advance decisions as to how you want your finances to function so that they will work well for you and your family.

The main idea in budgeting is for you to put aside a certain amount of money for expected as well as unexpected costs. The unexpected costs are usually the ones that most people leave out of their budget.

So, it is very important to make sure that you leave allowances for unexpected things such as car repair, home repair or anything else that may arise.

Simply put, budgeting means an estimation of monthly home expenses basing it on previous expenses and bills.

The initial step to take in budgeting is to find out how long will your compensation (funds) will last. First define fixed expenses like car payments, home rental, insurance, etc. Likewise follow up your expenditures thoroughly for a month so you can discover and understand where your funds are going. Through proper determination of your "spending patterns", you can immediately identify solutions for effective budgeting.

For instance, when you have a steady monthly income of $4,000, you should subtract all your identified monthly bills from that income first. Other bills can then be assessed and then subtracted from the amount of your income. The balance that remains after fixed costs can now be your budget in the household. Rather than allocating money for miscellaneous things like gas, clothing, entertainment and groceries, financial planning will allow you instead to use proportions or percentages of it.

The strategic solution in order for budgeting to be successful is inflexibility as well as flexibility; there are fixed expenses so payment must be an inflexible factor.

The whole idea here is to formulate goals and plans, and then abide by it as much as you possibly can.

With that in mind here are some quick tips on how to budget properly:

1. A good attitude is essential. Learn to have a good sense of money management. Once you plan your budget and understand that you have to make compromises and that it involves a lot of sacrifice to reduce your expenditures and stick to your budget, you will Begin to see the benefits and rewards that go along with a good budget.

2. Plan for every situation. Make a logbook with your earnings listed to one side and your overheads on the other side. Good record-keeping is essential to any good budget.

3. Learn the difference between luxuries and necessities. This is very important. Make a list of what you think are luxuries such as jewelry, fancy restaurants an extra pair of stylish shoes that you

see in the shop window and refer back to it every time you get tempted to spend outside of your budget.

4. Practice frugality without extreme denial. Remember you can have fun with little or no spending at all. Try this, rather than going shopping, play with your kids at the park or meet a friend for a walk on the beach. The point is there are many things you can do that won't cost you a dime and you may even enjoy them more.

Budgeting is an effective and fundamental tool that should be included in to your daily life. Setting up and sticking to a good budget will not only help you to save money, it will also help you relieve stress that comes from being overextended.

Finally Take Charge

With prices increasing and income decreasing day by day, it is very important to make your very own strategic plan so that you can maximize your financial resources and making sure that every penny you will earn is well spent.

There is no better time than now to make your move to start coordinating your finances and listing your expenditures. By taking the time to assess and set up a good budget will dramatically affect the way you use your income as well as empower you on your Way to economic stability.

There are many factors that need to be included in a good budgeting plan. For instance your source of income, lifestyle, spending habits, current job, location, cost of living, debts and loans all determine your level of budgeting needs. Taking charge of your finances is the only sure way of becoming successful, self-fulfilled and successful.

I have put together a few tips and recommendations that will provide you with some details on how you can successfully manage your finances and assume a new outlook on budgeting so that you can become responsible in your spending.

1. Treat Math As Your Lifetime Partner – Take the time to do the math when it comes to your purchasing needs. For instance, when you are grocery shopping or purchasing household items take the time to comparison shop before you leave the house.

This will save you money in more ways than one.

2. Do your best to save as much as you can on any item you plan to buy? You can do this in many different ways. For instance, you can purchase certain items in bulk, use coupons, and look for specials or for larger purchases call around for the best sales and prices before you leave the house. Every little thing you do will help you effectively budget your money.

3. Don't gamble – Did you know that gambling tops the chart in making your life chaotic and stressful. Gambling not only strips you of your finances it keeps you vulnerable to the threat of legal action from creditors and may also result in bankruptcy over the long term. There is no faster way to lose your hard earned income than to gamble it away.

4. Know your wants and needs – Limit your spending to things that you really need, not to things that you simply want. According to a recent study, luxuries are second to gambling in terms of the degree of money-stripping capability. It's okay to want just make sure you plan ahead to purchase the things that you want, and that the purchased doesn't send you over your budget and put you into debt.

5. Don't spend more than you earn – This is a big one. It is a trap that many of us easily fall into. Just keep in mind that you cannot live in a world where you consume more than what you can produce.

6. Keep a list – Making your own budget list is very important to your budgeting success. Keep in mind that a wise buyer needs to consider the amount of a certain purchase and how will it impact their life as an individual before they make a purchase. Take the time to think before you buy and living within your budget will be much easier.

After all an un conscientious consumer may not care about what is being purchased as long as he or she has money to spend, but for those that don't have a considerable amount of wealth and income resources it is important to create and stick to a good budget.

Chapter 4- Outline a Financial Budget Calendar

For some, the idea of a creating budget is often a confusing blur.

Once you decide to create a budget it can be frustrating to see how hard it is to create and stick to a budget. For some the realization that with one wrong purchase, you can ruin the entire thing keeps them from making a budget at all.

Isn't it about time to overhaul the way you think about budgeting?

It can actually be a great way to keep track of your family's expenditures and help you evaluate the things that you spend the major part of your family's earnings on.

I know we have discussed this before but have you ever asked yourself the question, exactly what is a budget?

Let's do a quick recap:

A budget is a tool for handling your finances by controlling the family's expenditures in a way that there is enough money for paying up bills, and still ensuring that savings are set aside for future expenses like vacations, children's education, or even for your retirement.

I want you to try these simple steps the next time you are preparing your family budget, and see if these no fret tips will help make the job easier.

1. Gather three months of your pay stubs and calculate your average monthly earnings.

2. Get out three months of your monthly bills. Do this for the fixed expenses like the rent, phone bill, car payments and other loans that come every month. Add them up and get the average. Do the same for other expenses like groceries, credit card bills and essentials.

3. Evaluate the results of your calculations. Take a good look at your average monthly earnings against your monthly fixed expenses and other monthly expenses, think of some ways to economize.

Cut back on some items that is somehow unnecessary.

4. Once you know the facts of your income and expenses you can develop a family budget and do your best to stick to it every month.

5. Now that you have a monthly budget, set up a savings account. Save up by making regular deposits to this account. Even if you can

only save a few dollars from each paycheck, it is very important to start developing good saving habits.

6. Keep track of your monthly family budget just to see if it is working for you. Don't get upset, if at first, you are unable to adhere to your new budget. You will find that you will have to fine-tune the "rough edges" of your budget as you go along. Remember practice makes perfect!

7. If possible use personal budgeting software or a spreadsheet application to keep record of your budget. Once you get the hang of keeping your budget this way, you will find that it makes organizing your expenses very easy.

These are the basic steps in developing and implementing a no fret, easy to stick to monthly family budget. Of course each family has diverse needs and wants. Just keep in mind that you have the freedom to develop your own monthly family budget, depending on your family's financial background and needs. No matter how you do it, just focus on the end result, which is building a savings that leads to a bright and financially stable future for you and your family.

Budgeting Software

The problem with most people these days is that they get so comfortable with their expenses through the aid of credit cards.

They become so indulged with cash less shopping that more and more people are spending more than what they can afford.

For this reason, experts contend that budgeting can definitely alleviate the consumers from "financial strain" by managing their expenses and income instead of falling into the pit of liabilities.

However, some people just contend that they cannot simply manage their budgeting alone. They insist that they need some help in order to come up with a reliable and workable budget.

That's why some financial experts have created money budgeting software that will help you in the creation of a good budget in order to promote wise money-saving strategies.

Basically, money budgeting software aids you in keeping track of your expenditures and helps you learn how to spend your money sensibly. This will you help distribute your money into various aspects and areas and will also help add to your savings.

Let's quickly go over some of the advantages of using budgeting software.

1. It helps you keep track of your expenses.

Money budgeting software can definitely allow you to keep track of your expenses. With this kind of technology, you get to understand your cash flow and allow you to be aware of how much money you spend and earn.

2. It helps you to create some probable projections of the future.

While some people are comfortable with the usual type of budgeting on paper, utilizing money budgeting software can give you more than what you expect. You can even make some possible projections using your integrated money budgeting software. And if you are really into hard copies, you can even print them out for record keeping.

3. It gives you control.

The problem with most people who do not have a budget in place to guide them is that they usually tend to overspend what money they do have. Using software can help you gain control of your expenditures. You will be able to know ahead of time before it's too late, and you've spent more than your budget allows.

The bottom line is that money budgeting software can definitely give you the kind of assurance and control that you need to keep track of your expenses. In this way, you can be sure that all of your spending activities are based on careful planning and reasonable thought, not just sheer indulgences.

Tips for Budget Planning

Tell me are you the lucky one in charge of creating the family budget? If you are then chances this are you've had the unfortunate experience of having a brilliant budget plan that isn't executed well. Don't worry this happens to many families and couples.

It's important to keep in mind that if your budget doesn't work as smoothly as you had hoped in the beginning that you keep a good attitude and do a little tweaking. Remember you're not alone in this; you can solicit the help of your family when it comes to making your budget work.

The first thing you should do is sit down together and create a family budget vision. Talk to your spouse and children about whatever budgetary constraints you are facing, or whatever financial goals you plan to achieve. By being completely honest about the expenses that you have to pay, your intentions to save a certain amount of money for the family emergency fund or your child's college fund you can help your family understand your financial situation better. This will allow them to change their perspective on purchases they make. It will also help you make sure that whatever money crunching strategies you utilize won't be counteracted by an in prompt to shopping spree by your spouse or teen.

Another good technique is to create a list of usual expenditures for each member of your family. Together, identify which items you can do away with in order to save up some extra money from your monthly income. By doing this together, you are making your family a part of the budgeting process. This will also allow them to see the contributions that they can make as an individual and understand how working together will make your family's financial situation better.

Should your child have the habit of continuously asking for money for minor and oftentimes unnecessary purchases, you can let your children learn to manage their own week's allowance. With their own limited money to budget. By doing this they will realize the real value of money.

Put a cap on the amount of expenditures you make in a week.

The best way to do this is set aside a fixed amount of cash that you will spend each week. By putting this limitation on your spending, you are forced to prioritize your spending on the things that are most essential over other things that are not.

Make it easy for your family to save more. Tell me, how often do you and your family eat out? Did you know that most family budgets are blown simply because of the frequency and expense of dining out? Eating at home will reduce your expenses tremendously, not to mention allow your family to spend more time together. Try it for a week or two you'll be amazed at how much money you'll save and how much you'll enjoy it!

Do you spend more than you need to on routine purchases like coffee and newspapers? I know you may not seem like much when you spend a dollar for coffee and a quarter for a paper but these small purchases really adds up. Try this for a month, cut back on the latte and the paper. Then put aside the amount you would normally spend on these daily purchases. If everyone in your family does this your collective savings will surprise you.

Lastly, don't ignore your driving habits. Try to group your family activities together into one car trip and eliminate unnecessary trips to the store. I know this might sound a bit extreme, but with the high cost of gas and other car expenses you will be amazed at how much money you can save just by carpooling.

CHAPTER 5- MIND SETTING ON EFFECTIVE MONEY-SAVING

Did you know that saving is your best defense against bankruptcy?

Bankruptcy is a very scary prospect that most average income people hope they never have to face, but if you include a plan to save it will insulate you from possible financial loss and give you the ability to expand your finances and create a money generating budgeting machine that will help you stay on top of your finances.

The basic idea of planning is to save while creating your budget focus on spending less than what you earn and keeping something extra for future use and for unforeseen circumstances.

Today we're going to go over some ways that you can effectively maximize your financial resources and manage your money by developing good saving habits, so that you can reach your goals.

First let's talk about wants and needs – We all buy items because we feel we need them, right? A need is something that can't be taken away, because our very existence depends on them.

For instance: food, shelter, clothing and transportation are the primary examples of things that are needed to function in today's society. Even cell phones and electronic gadgets are a necessary part of a busy individuals work day.

This is where some people get confused. They often justify a want as a need and this leads to excess spending.

Let's consider this; if you are receiving less than $10,000 a month, chances are you don't need to have a $50,000 luxury vehicle. The same can be said for other things as well, like having your own cell phone. We know in most cases, this is necessary but, what isn't necessary it is keeping up with the latest model or purchasing every gadget and gizmo that goes along with the cell phone just to be trendy.

It is important to learn how to identify the difference between something that you really need versus something that you simply want.

Have you ever heard the phrase "less is best"? While we all enjoy pampering ourselves from time to time with things like dinner out, new clothes, a piece of jewelry or maybe a massage, we also need to consider that these types of activities should only be reserved for special occasions and for times when you have planned ahead, or have excess money left in your household budget.

Chances are when you were growing up your parents said this to you. Spend Less and Save More! Spending more than what you earn is a trap that many people fall into everyday without even being aware of what they're doing until it's too late. It's important when you create your budget to allocate a special percentage of your earnings to go into your savings accounts while spending the rest for your day-to-day expenses. This way, when unexpected expenses pop up like an impromptu visit from your favorite relative, and overdue bill or an unexpected trip out of town you will be prepared and your budget will not suffer.

I hope that this is helped you understand why it is so important to include a plan to save when you are creating your budget. Often times, the family budget is a source of conflict. Most of the time, the major earner makes the final financial decision, which isn't always a welcome deal for the rest of the family.

Since money is such a big part of part of family life, families need to work together to reach their budgeting goals.

There is a four-step cycle in budgeting the family money to maintain peace and harmony.

1. Set your priorities.

Here is a quick definition of priority. A priority is something that is given or meriting attention before competing alternatives.

Simply put, the things that you feel are most important are prioritized and put at the top of the list when you are creating your budget.

Priorities are different from goals. They are aspects in your family's life that you, as a family, want to set focus on, for instance health care, retirement or your children's college fund.

When you start setting priorities be careful not set too many as it will defeat the purpose. Ideally, there should only be one, but because life is not ideal, 2 to 3 are reasonable.

As the priorities are set and agreed upon, write them down. Post the paper where everybody can see them to remind them of what your family is focused on for the next few years or until that goal is reached.

2. List down your goals.

Once the family has set and agreed on priorities, the next step is to set the goals. Goals are specific and measurable conditions that, when achieved, will support the priorities.

When setting goals, establish a target that is both challenging and achievable. For instance 10-15% of the family's income is a good savings target for your child's future education because it's challenging yet reachable.

When you are setting your goals try to limit your family into setting 1 or 2 goals for each priority, so that you can all maintain focus.

3. Work towards your goals.

After setting your priorities and goals, start living by them. All of the family's activities will be geared towards working to achieve your goals. Track progress, particularly on financial goals, by using an income and expense-tracking tool. The simplest way is to get a notebook and list down all expenses and incomes and set a budget for future spending or as we've discussed before use budgeting software. Whatever it is, the important thing is to have a system of monitoring the family's performance towards achieving their goals.

4. Evaluate your family life.

At a certain point in time, when you feel like it's time to evaluate your life, check how your family is doing against the goals. Goals that have been achieved can be checked off the list, and new ones can be formulated.

There will be times when major changes, say a career move, or when a family member moves away that it may be time to re-evaluate your family's priorities. When such a time occurs, then the cycle will begin all over again.

Emergency Funds

Emergency funds are considered to be a necessity as far as financial security is concerned, since it can provide you and your family with financial resources that you can resort to and depend on when an emergency arises, such as illness, medical bills, or unexpected home or major car repair.

What happens if you don't have an emergency fund in place?

You will be held responsible for the debt; whether it is a loan or on your credit card and the end result will be that it could take several years to repay with interest that will end up costing you so much more in the end.

However, by putting an extra thirty to fifty dollars every month in an individual "emergency savings account" you can be secure in knowing that you are prepared for any emergency that the future may bring. To make this easier on yourself just think of the emergency fund as an additional bill included in your budget that needs to be paid each month.

It is a very important to set up your budget, and allocate extra money for the family emergency fund. It is a very significant part of planning your family's financial future. Keep in mind the goal is to create savings from budgeting your income. Ideally your goal should be to have your emergency savings fund be equal to at least three months your living expenditures.

Another important thing to remember about your emergency savings fund besides putting funds into each month, is that it should only be used for actual emergencies and not that new pair of Italian shoes you think you'll die without.

In spite of your financial status, the initial step in the process building your family emergency fund is by knowing exactly where all of your money is presently being spent.

When you determine where your earnings are being spent, then it will be easy for you to decide where to trim down expenses to create your emergency savings fund.

As we've talked about before budgeting is simply setting aside money for anticipated and unanticipated future use.

The amount saved from budgeting can either go to your savings goal, emergency fund or both. You can utilize the money saved from budgeting your family's financial expenses by saving half of it to your savings account and half of it to your emergency fund. This way, you achieve your goals in savings and at the same time put in funds away for emergency use.

CHAPTER 6- FINANCIAL BUDGET WITH RETURN OF INCOME

Budgeting your monthly expenses in order to get the greatest return on your income (and perhaps, even put aside some for saving!) doesn't have to be painfully hard.

I know we have talked about budgeting software programs before, but I feel it needs mention again, because budgeting software is a tool that can really make your job easier.

There are various budgeting programs are available, from a simple to spreadsheet done with Excel to software like QuickBooks that will manage your personal finances or even your small business finances. Most money management programs provide you with a usual package that allows you to enter your cash inflows and outflows, categorizes your expenditures, and some even give you an analysis of your spending behavior.

With these programs you can also input the various payments you have to make monthly, and subsequently track if you've paid your bills on time. Some programs also offer you a tax form draft that will help you make sure you're not missing out on any dues or any deductibles. Be sure when you choose your software that you find one that suits your families needs the best.

Another budgeting tool that you can utilize is coupons. Don't laugh, there is a reason that your grandmother sat at the kitchen table and clipped coupons for hours at a time.

When you use coupons to purchase things that you need you will be surprised at how much money you can actually save. So take the time to search through the newspaper and magazines for coupons on products that you use regularly. Many times, grocery stores will even provide you with coupons in store, or that can be printed out online.

The only important thing to remember is not to buy something just because you have a coupon for it. Only buy things that you really need and if you have a coupon for them all the better.

Let's move on to lists. Whether you keep it on a piece of paper, on your computer, or on your personal digital assistant (PDA) lists will help you keep focused on what you have to buy, and in effect, keep track of the purchases you make.

A classic example....

Your regular trip to the grocery store. Before you go plan out the week's entire menu and identify what food items and ingredients that you'll need to purchase, that you don't already have. Then, make a list of other household items that you've run out of (or are eventually going to run out of before you can make your next trip to the grocery store). Armed with these lists, you can go to the grocery store and know exactly what you're going to buy. Without these lists, you will walk idly along aisles, and will most likely pick up items that you don't need, or already have at home, which will lead to spending more than your budget has allowed for.

A filing system is perhaps one of the best budgeting tools you can have in your home. With simple, labeled file folders, you can put together your bills, your receipts, and whatever bank documents are issued to you when you save or pay. By putting together your bills, your credit card receipts, and other records, you are able to keep track of how much you owe and when your payments are due.

Effective budgeting tools are those that best address your needs as a family and a consumer. You can create your own budgeting system or find a program to do it for you. Whichever ways you decide to keep track of your budget just make sure it suits your lifestyle.

Learn and Teach How to Save Money

A lot of teens nowadays do not understand the value of earning and spending money. They were not oriented that investing is necessary even if they are still students. As parents, you play a crucial role in this area.

You should be able to teach your kids on how to save money. They should be able to understand the concept of money and investments as early as childhood. This will prepare them to learn money management, as they grow older.

Here are some tips on how you can teach your children how to save money:

1. Your children should be educated of the meaning of money. Once your children have learned how to count, that is the perfect time for you teach them the real meaning of money.

You should be consistent and explain to them in simple ways and do this frequently so that they may be able to remember what you taught them.

2. Always explain to them the value of saving money. Make them understand its importance and how it will impact their life. It is important that you entertain questions from them about money and you should be able to answer them right away.

3. When giving them their allowances. You need to give them their allowances in denominations. Then you can encourage them that they should keep a certain bill for the future. You can motivate them to do this by telling them that the money can be saved and they can buy new pair of shoes or the toys they want once they are able to save.

4. You can also teach them to work for money. You can start this at your own home. You can pay them fifty cents to one dollar every time they clean their rooms, do the dishes or feed their pets. This concept of earning little money will make them think that money is something they have worked for and should be spent wisely.

5. You can teach them to save money by giving them piggy banks where they can put coins and wait until they get full. You can also open bank accounts for them and let them deposit money from their allowance. You should always show them how much they have earned to keep them motivated.

Money and saving is not something that is learned by children in one sitting. You should be patient in teaching them and relating the value of money in all of their activities. Children will learn this easily if you are patient and consistent in guiding them and encouraging them in this endeavor.

10 Practical Ways to Save

Saving money is not as hard as it seems. Here are ten practical tips that you can use to begin saving money, without changing your lifestyle.

1. Replace incandescent bulbs with compact fluorescent (CFL) bulbs. CFL bulbs consume 80% less energy than incandescent bulbs, but give the same illumination. Make sure to buy only lamps and bulbs that have the Energy Star rating to ensure quality compliance.

2. Make a list when going to the grocery and stick to it! Anything that is not on the list is not a "need", but merely a "want "so avoid spending money on unnecessary items. When possible buy non-perishable consumables in bulk to benefit from bulk discounts.

3. Use coupons when available. Take the time and have the patience to clip and organize grocery coupons. When added together, savings from using all coupons in one grocery trip can be as much as $20-$30. Purchase dining and shopping coupons online and print them at home. Doing so can save you at least 50% on the face value of the coupons.

4. Buy online, whenever possible. Online stores pass their savings from rental costs and warehousing to the online consumer, thus they can afford as much as 70% off their rack price. When buying items online, Google it first together with the word, "discount

code". This can give you further reductions on the item you want to purchase. Try also online bidding: they offer at least 75% off the original purchase price, for practically new (slightly used!) items.

5. Take lunch to work. Buy potato chips and soda from the grocery and make a homemade sandwich and pack them in a brown bag.

6. Eat homemade dinners as often as possible. Plan menus that are practical and easy-to-cook to encourage eating at home. Save money by dining out only on special occasions.

7. Use everyday pantry items for skin and body care.

Cucumbers, honey, milk, lemon, salt and baking soda are some items in your home that can also be used to take care of your skin.

8. Avoid shopping to de-stress.

Try walking around the park or watching a movie instead.

9. Bring your own sodas and snacks when watching a movie. The cost of sodas and snacks are at least 25% higher in movie houses. Plus, homemade popcorn tastes much better: you can put on all the salt and butter you want!

10. Pay off your credit card balances each month and avoid finance charges. Better yet, use cash as much as possible, unless using plastic will give you a better deal (0% interest on appliance purchases, or cash rebates).

CHAPTER 7- GO FOR PIGGY BANK THEORY

For most people going into the work force today there is very little possibility of being able to enjoy some sort of pension plans as these plans are becoming more "extinct".

Such pension plan facilities are no longer a requirement or a compulsory addition to an individual's salary deductions. Therefore without such allowances in place for retirement the individual would be wise to start a saving plan to accommodate the retirement phase of his or her life.

Learning to lock in a certain amount as soon as possible towards a savings plan will allow the individual to plan accordingly, thus ensuring this said sum is systematically allotted.

Making this a habit that comes naturally will help to make the entire saving exercise both easy and accepted. It will also allow the individual to work round other financial commitments to ensure the savings contributions are not effected in any way.

Besides this the individual will learn to be disciplined and thus create a comfortable spending habit from a very early on age. The percentage of the savings should also be increased according to the job advancements made.

This would ensure the savings amount becomes healthier which in turn would ensure a more comfortable retirement phase.

Investing in suitable savings plans will also allow the individual to make tax relief claims which should work as an incentive to save even more or provide the funds to invest even more towards a suitable retirement plan.

Don't Save and Spend. Save and Invest

If an individual is only going to depend on a savings plan for retirement, the eventual amounts saved may not be nearly enough to support a comfortable retirement phase as the inflations and value of the money will definitely be lesser as time goes on.

Therefore there is a serious need to look towards investing in other tools that may provide comfortable returns that would add on to the savings plan in place.

The following are some recommendations on other possible areas that should be explored with the intention of creating investment plans for retirement:

Investment planning – this area can provide the individual with platforms where the money works on fetching a better than average interest earnings by planning the investments at the right time and choice. These usually provide with good return on the values over time.

Real estate investment – real estate investments is all about committing funds to entities, such as various forms of properties that will eventually yield suitable income earning revenue for the individual. There may come in the form of rentals, leases and proper deals, where the properties bought can be sold for very good profits.

These are all ways to create suitable savings possibilities.

Bonds and securities investment plans – these can bring about effective investment growth that will eventually contribute toward the funds that can secure a comfortable retirement phase for the individual. The long term investments may come in the form of bonds such as life assurance and death policies. Besides this there are also possibilities investing in government bonds and other entities.

Endowment policies – these are also another very good option to take up in the quest to create a comfortable savings platform to retirement. Paying towards such plans early on, will create an ideal source on income eventually.

401K and IRA

These are two very powerful savings tools that are becoming more popular as more working adults opt for such plans. The assurance of having money put away for retirement through these secure platforms will encourage those not yet doing so to seriously consider these options.

A 401k plan is basically a scenario where the company the individual is currently working for, offers, as part of its remuneration package a percentage based on the salary amounts to be paid on behalf of the individual, toward this account on a monthly basis.

These amounts are then accumulated plus interest to provide for the retirement phase of the individual. The lock in period for this type of saving plan is also another advantage as the individual will have no access to the amounts in the account until retirement age is reached, thus effectively keeping the money safe from unnecessary seeming important spending sprees for the individual.

IRA investments usually come in two forms which are traditional and Roth. However both are compatible to a retired persons needs as serves as a good investing tool.

The traditional IRA is done in a more independent manner which for some is a better option, as they get to dictate the investment amount and how to invest.

There is also the advantage of the amount being partially tax deductible depending on the plan chosen. The difference here is that there is a possibility of withdrawing some amounts before the actual retirement age but this is then subject to certain taxation issues.

Upon retirement there is also a tax on the amounts withdrawn though it is quite minimal.

For early withdrawal there is also a penalty charged. As for the Roth IRA the similarities between the two are evident however there are also some differences. One of which is the Roth style is not subject to tax deductions upon retirements as the tax is deducted on the amounts are deposited and taken at that time.

CHAPTER 8- CONTROL FREAK OVER YOUR FINANCES

Recently there has been a lot of interest in this form of investment tool. The mutual fund investment platform presents an attractive alternative to savings toward a comfortable retirement. Besides saving towards retirement there are also other financial goals that can be effectively met through the mutual fund style of investing.

Mutual funds can most time offer the advantage of providing diversified and professional management, but this is done for a fee. As with other forms of investments there is a certain level of risk involved in the dabbling of mutual fund investments.

In some cases if the investment does not pan out as first anticipated or expected, there are fees and taxes incurred that will make the whole exercise quite disadvantages and also end up being the cause of the diminishing in fund returns.

Therefore in the quest to ensure optimum benefits are derived from this type of investment there has to be some level of understanding, by the investor about the downsides and the upsides of the mutual fund investing tool.

The prospective investor should have some sound knowledge about how the mutual funds work, what factors should be considered when researching for possible investments, how to avoid pitfalls and problems and any other information that might have an impact on the choices made.

Some of these factors may include the degree of risks involved both in the long term and short term style for the mutual funds chosen, the strategies involved in making such decisions and how to ensure these decisions are made based on sound knowledge, the fees and expenses that are normally incurred through the investing process and some of the terms and labels used to describe the various levels and connotations linked to the mutual fund itself.

The main idea behind choosing the mutual fund investment is to ensure the retirement plan is well served by this form of savings.

Appreciate Frugal Living

Living frugally does not necessarily mean living in poverty or having to constantly deprive one's self of the finer things in life. Depriving one's self of anything and everything is not what the frugal living lifestyle is all about. In fact it is just the opposite, because with frugal living the individual is able to keep expenses low, pay off debts faster, save and invest comfortably.

The following are explanations on how to "marry" the two factors while still being able to enjoy a fairly pleasant lifestyle that is neither deprivative nor depressing:

Learning to be comfortable with smaller size elements that work well and are equally compatible with the individual's lifestyle.

Although it may seem nice to have everything is large sizes, from houses to cars to holidays to spending allowances, with a little bit or knowledge and research anyone can find smaller yet suitably tailor elements that are equally if not better.

Therefore going big always may not only seem a wasteful opulence it can also lead to huge debts.

For some leasing or renting may present a more financially attractive package than actually owning. This is due to the fact that when there is ownership issues involved, all expenses and cost are born by the owner itself, and these hidden costs can be quite substantial.

Therefore with the savings from all these hidden expenses and cost that come from ownership, the individual can look for good investment opportunities that may bring about an even better financial standing.

When it comes to eating expenses, most individuals do not really realize just how much can be saved and how to go about making these adjustments to procure the intended savings. Eating frugally yet healthily is one way of keeping the expenses in check. Taking the trouble to fix meals at home is more cost effective that going out to eat all the time.

Financial Help from Financial Adviser

With so many options available to make good investments it can be quite confusing for the individual who is not savvy and does not possess the important elements it takes to be a good and sound investor.

The various investment opportunities available, also comes with a lot of confusing jargon, that the individual may not be able to relate to, thus causing further confusion and maybe even contributing to some poor judgment calls.

Most people are busy with the everyday routines and distractions, that sparing the time and energy to delve into the mostly confusing financial investment opportunities is really not an option that can be fully explored. Although some may take the plunge, most would rather engage the services of a reputable financial advisor who would be able to completely concentrate on finding the best investment opportunities for the client.

As these financial advisors are more knowledgeable on the various sorts of investment tools available, their opinions would be better accepted. Most financial advisers depend very much on the recommendations of satisfied clients, to expand their portfolios of customers, thus being experienced and good investment advisors is part of their attention grabbing tools.

Financial advisors are also trained to help an individual plan and budget according to their financial capabilities and this can be useful to an individual who is currently not able to enjoy or capitalize, on his or her own financial standing.

Making money and losing money today can be a life changing or life threatening experience. For some the challenge of being able to dictate their own financial journey is important, while for others a little help may be not only necessary but perhaps even compulsory. Here is when the services of a financial adviser could prove to be an advantage worth taking.

ABOUT THE AUTHOR

Katherine Owens is a known personal finance commentator and journalist. She is currently into writing books especially made for parents. Katherine is also a regular lecturer on financial literacy, public policy issues, and consumer finance. She has worked extensively with different insurance company and also promotes credit card awareness to different organization.

Katherine is married to Alfred and they have a lovely daughter named Sophia.

www.ingramcontent.com/pod-product-compliance
Lightning Source LLC
Chambersburg PA
CBHW051250170526
45165CB00004B/1657